THE 19TH AMENDMENT

LAURA LORIA

Mr. PRESIDENT
HOW LONG
MUST
WOMEN WAIT
FOR LIBERTY

Britannica®
Educational Publishing

IN ASSOCIATION WITH

ROSEN
EDUCATIONAL SERVICES
NASHVILLE PUBLIC LIBRARY

Published in 2017 by Britannica Educational Publishing (a trademark of Encyclopædia Britannica, Inc.) in association with The Rosen Publishing Group, Inc.
29 East 21st Street, New York, NY 10010

Distributed exclusively by Rosen Publishing.
To see additional Britannica Educational Publishing titles, go to rosenpublishing.com.

First Edition

Britannica Educational Publishing
J.E. Luebering: Executive Director, Core Editorial
Mary Rose McCudden: Editor, Britannica Student Encyclopedia

Rosen Publishing
Nicholas Croce and Amelie von Zumbusch: Editors
Nelson Sá: Art Director
Nicole Russo: Designer
Cindy Reiman: Photography Manager

Library of Congress Cataloging-in-Publication Data

Names: Loria, Laura, author.
Title: The 19th Amendment / Laura Loria.
Other titles: Nineteenth Amendment
Description: First edition. | New York : Britannica Educational Publishing in
  association with Rosen Educational Services, 2017. | Series: Let's find
  out! Primary sources | Includes bibliographical references and index.
Identifiers: LCCN 2016020887 | ISBN 9781508104018 (library bound : alk. paper)
  | ISBN 9781508104025 (pbk. : alk. paper) | ISBN 9781508103226 (6-pack :
  alk. paper)
Subjects: LCSH: Women—Suffrage—United States—History—Juvenile literature.
  | United States. Constitution. 19th Amendment—History—Juvenile
  literature.
Classification: LCC KF4895 .L67 2017 | DDC 324.6/230973—dc23
LC record available at https://lccn.loc.gov/2016020887

Manufactured in China

Photo Credits: Cover, p. 1 Everett Historical/Shutterstock.com; p. 4 Library of Congress Rare Book and Special Collections Division Washington, D.C.; pp. 5, 10, 11, 12, 14, 16, 18, 22, 24, 25 Library of Congress Prints and Photographs Division, Washington, D.C.; p. 6 Print Collector/Hulton Archive/Getty Images; p. 7 De Agostini Picture Library/Bridgeman Images; pp. 8, 21, 23 Encyclopædia Britannica, Inc.; p. 9 Universal History Archive/Universal Images Group/Getty Images; p. 13 Bettmann/Getty Images; pp. 15, 19 Courtesy of the Department of Rare Books, Special Collections and Preservation, University of Rochester River Campus Libraries; p. 17 Brady-Handy Photograph Collection/Library of Congress, Washington, D.C. (LC-DIG-cwpbh-03892); p. 20 David Boyer/National Geographic Image Collection/Getty Images; p. 26 Photos.com/Thinkstock; p. 27 Zohra Bensemra/Reuters/Landov; p. 28 © AP Images; p. 29 Joe Amon/The Denver Post/Getty Images; interior pages background image Tischenko Irina/Shutterstock.com.

CONTENTS

THE REAL DEAL

How do authors of books on history know what happened? The best information about events from the past comes from primary sources. These are documents and other things that come from the time period a **historian** is researching. They also come from the people involved in the event. Primary sources can be newspaper articles, photographs, diaries, paintings, and more.

Primary sources are often more accurate than accounts that were written later. As time passes, people forget exactly how and when events

Newspapers are excellent primary sources for learning about events from the past.

4

◀◀

Women had to fight for years before gaining the right to vote.

occurred. Primary sources also tell how individual people felt about an event when it happened.

One of the many topics in history that we can learn about from primary sources is the long fight for women's suffrage, or the right to vote. In 1920 the 19th Amendment to the United States Constitution finally granted American women suffrage. Amendments are changes or additions to the Constitution.

Women's Work

In the past, a woman was expected to care only about her home and family.

In many countries today women have the same rights as men. They have the right to own property. They have the right to get an education. They have the right to work at any job they choose. They have the  right to vote. But it has not always been this way.

In the past, a woman's work was her home life. She did all of the cooking, cleaning, and childcare. Her husband was responsible for working to support the family.

COMPARE AND CONTRAST

What roles do women have today? How is it different now from how it was in the past?

Some women became powerful leaders, such as Cleopatra in ancient Egypt and Queen Elizabeth I in England. However, most women had few rights of their own. Many laws were written with the word "men" instead of "people," so they didn't apply to women. Women knew that if they were going to change society they must win suffrage, or the right to vote. In this way they could take part in government. Then they could influence policies and laws.

For many years, wives did not have equal rights with their husbands.

7

The Birth of a Movement

Many women were dissatisfied with their lack of rights, but only a few brave women were able to do something about it. In the United States, Elizabeth Cady Stanton, Lucretia Mott, and several other women got together. They decided to hold a meeting for women in 1848. While they were planning this meeting, they wrote out their ideas.

This document was called the "Declaration of

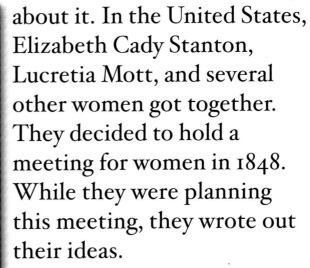

Lucretia Mott helped to begin the movement for women's rights.

THINK ABOUT IT

Why might it have been difficult for women to attend the convention?

This pamphlet from the convention has parts of the speeches given that day.

Sentiments." It describes how women were unfairly treated. It also demands that they be seen as equals to men. It says, "...woman is man's equal...she should be recognized as such."

Although Stanton and her friends planned the meeting with only five days' notice, around 200 people attended, mainly women. It was called the Women's Rights Convention, and it was held in Seneca Falls, New York.

THE FIRST CONVENTION

EVER CALLED TO DISCUSS THE

Civil and Political Rights of Women,

SENECA FALLS, N. Y., JULY 19, 20, 1848.

———

WOMAN'S RIGHTS CONVENTION.

———

A Convention to discuss the social, civil, and religious condition and rights of woman will be held in the Wesleyan Chapel, at Seneca Falls, N. Y., on Wednesday and Thursday, the 19th and 20th of July current; commencing at 10 o'clock A. M. During the first day the meeting will be exclusively for women, who are earnestly invited to attend. The public generally are invited to be present on the second day, when Lucretia Mott, of Philadelphia, and other ladies and gentlemen, will address the Convention.*

———————————————————————
* This call was published in the *Seneca County Courier*, July 14, 1848, without any signatures. The movers of this Convention, who drafted the call, the declaration and resolutions were Elizabeth Cady Stanton, Lucretia Mott, Martha C. Wright, Mary Ann McClintock, and Jane C. Hunt.

THE MOVEMENT GROWS

The success of the 1848 convention inspired Stanton and Mott to plan more meetings. The next meeting was held in Worcester, Massachusetts, in October 1850. It was called the National Woman's Rights Convention.

At the convention, speakers such as Lucy Stone called for women to be given the right to vote. More than one thousand people attended. Newspaper reporters came as well, to record the events. Many of them mocked the

Lucy Stone spoke out for the rights of women and African Americans.

women. They did not take them seriously. The *New York Tribune* published a letter from one gentleman, who wrote, "Now, if women are given the right to vote, ...the dinners must go *un*cooked, the children's faces *un*washed, and home be forgotten..."

The women felt that even negative attention was good for their **cause.** Interest in women's rights was growing. There were conventions like this nearly every year for the rest of the decade.

Early suffragist Paulina Davis led the 1850 convention.

VOCABULARY

A **cause** is an idea that a person supports.

Rights for All

At this time in American history, women weren't the only people who did not have rights. Slavery was still legal, and African Americans were not able to vote either. Many people who supported women's suffrage were also abolitionists, or people who were against slavery.

One former slave, Sojourner Truth, spoke up at the Woman's Convention in Akron, Ohio, in 1851. Truth argued that she was

Sojourner Truth's "Ain't I a Woman?" speech is still well known today.

COMPARE AND CONTRAST

Do you think that slaves and women had similar struggles when trying to get equal rights?

as strong as a man, and should be treated equally. She repeated the phrase, "Ain't I a woman?" to make her point, and that is what her speech came to be called.

African American men gained the right to vote with the 15th Amendment to the Constitution in 1870. Many women were upset that they weren't included in the new law.

Like women, African American men had to fight to win the right to vote.

SPREADING THE WORD

To promote their cause, Elizabeth Cady Stanton and Susan B. Anthony, another women's rights advocate, began a newspaper called *The Revolution* in 1868. It was printed every week for four years. It did not have many readers, but it was a very important part of women's history.

The Revolution became the official newspaper of the

Anthony, standing, and Stanton worked together to publish *The Revolution*.

National Woman Suffrage Association. That group was founded in 1869 by Stanton and Anthony. They worked to gain voting rights for women throughout the country. Other women founded the American Woman Suffrage Association at the same time. They tried to gain rights for women one state at a time. The two groups later combined to form the National American Woman Suffrage Association.

This issue of *The Revolution* featured a piece written by Paulina Davis.

THINK ABOUT IT

Why was it important for Stanton and Anthony to put their ideas in print?

The Revolution.

PRINCIPLE, NOT POLICY; JUSTICE, NOT FAVORS.—MEN, THEIR RIGHTS AND NOTHING MORE: WOMEN, THEIR RIGHTS AND NOTHING LESS.

VOL. I.—NO. IV.   NEW YORK, THURSDAY, JULY 8, 1869.   WHOLE NO. 79.

TAKING ACTION

At this time, some women across the nation had attempted to vote, but most did not succeed. The most famous attempt was that of Susan B. Anthony. She tried to vote in Rochester, New York, in 1872.

Four days before the election, Anthony, her three sisters, and a friend registered to vote. A lawyer who supported women's suffrage helped them. When Anthony voted on

Susan B. Anthony was willing to risk going to jail for her right to vote.

Judge Ward Hunt did not send Anthony to jail when she didn't pay her fine.

Election Day, she was featured in many newspapers. Unfortunately, she was arrested for her actions several weeks later.

At her **trial** months later, her lawyer argued that Anthony did not feel she was breaking the law. She was simply exercising her right to vote. The judge decided that Anthony's belief did "not protect her in the act which she committed." She was sentenced to pay a fine of $100, but she refused to pay.

VOCABULARY

A **trial** is the hearing and judgment of a case in court.

THE NATIONAL STAGE

The National Woman Suffrage Association continued on its quest to win the right of women to vote. The organization produced a pamphlet, or small booklet, called the "Declaration of Rights of the Women of the United States," in 1876.

The pamphlet was written for a celebration of the U.S. Centennial in Philadelphia, Pennsylvania. A centennial is the 100th anniversary of an event. July

Matilda Joslyn Gage was one of the authors of the "Declaration."

THINK ABOUT IT

Do you think reading the pamphlet out loud was more effective than printing it in the program?

4, 1876, was the centennial of the founding of the United States. The declaration expressed disappointment that, one hundred years after the nation was formed, women's rights had not advanced. It said, "woman's discontent [anger] has been steadily increasing" over many injustices. The document listed those injustices.

The association wanted the pamphlet to be printed in the event's program, but that did not happen. Instead, Susan B. Anthony boldly marched up to the platform where a senator was standing, handed him the pamphlet, and then read it aloud.

Susan B. Anthony read the "Declaration" on Independence Day, 1876.

DECLARATION OF RIGHTS
OF THE
WOMEN OF THE UNITED STATES
BY THE
NATIONAL WOMAN SUFFRAGE ASSOCIATION.
JULY 4th, 1876.

WHILE the Nation is buoyant with patriotism, and all hearts are attuned to praise, it is with sorrow we come to strike the one discordant note, on this hundredth anniversary of our country's birth. When subjects of Kings, Emperors, and Czars, from the Old World, join in our National Jubilee, shall the women of the Republic refuse to lay their hands with benedictions on the nation's head? Surveying America's Exposition, surpassing in magnificence those of London, Paris, and Vienna, shall we not rejoice at the success of the youngest rival among the nations of the earth? May not our hearts, in unison with all, swell with pride at our great achievements as a people; our free speech, free press, free schools, free church, and the rapid progress we have made in material wealth, trade, commerce, and the inventive arts? And we do rejoice, in the success thus far, of our experiment of self-government. Our faith is firm and unwavering in the broad principles of human rights, proclaimed in 1776, not only as abstract truths, but as the corner stones of a republic. Yet, we cannot forget, even in this glad hour, that while all men of every race, and clime, and condition, have been invested with the full rights of citizenship, under our hospitable flag, all women still suffer the degradation of disfranchisement.

The history of our country the past hundred years, has been a series of assumptions and usurpations of power over woman, in direct opposition to the principles of just government, acknowledged by the United States at its foundation, which are:

First. The natural rights of each individual.
Second. The exact equality of these rights.
Third. That these rights, when not delegated by the individual, are retained by the individual.
Fourth. That no person can exercise the rights of others without delegated authority.
Fifth. That the non-use of these rights does not destroy them.

And for the violation of these fundamental principles of our Government, we arraign our rulers on this 4th day of July, 1876,—and these are our

ARTICLES OF IMPEACHMENT.

BILLS OF ATTAINDER have been passed by the introducti... ll the State constitutions, denying to woman the right of suffrage, and thereby makin... wer clearly forbidden in Article 1st, Sections 9th and 10th of the United States Cons...

State by State

Histories of women's suffrage often focus on events that took place in the northeastern United States. However, one of the greatest advances occurred across the country, in Wyoming. Before it gained statehood, the Territory of Wyoming granted women the right to vote in 1869.

In order to become a state, Wyoming had to have a constitution. The people who wrote the constitution made sure to include a section saying

ESTHER HOBART MORRIS
PROPONENT OF THE LEGISLATIVE ACT WHICH IN 1869 GAVE DISTINCTION TO THE TERRITORY OF
WYOMING
AS THE 1ST GOVERNMENT IN THE WORLD TO GRANT WOMEN EQUAL RIGHTS

Esther Morris helped lead the fight for women's suffrage in Wyoming.

that women could vote. They also wrote that all people in the state should have the same rights, "without distinction of race, color, sex, or any circumstance or condition whatsoever." The United States Congress then had to vote to approve Wyoming's statehood. Some members of the Congress objected to the idea of women's suffrage. They were outvoted, and in 1890 Wyoming became a state. It was the first in the nation to have universal suffrage. Over the next few years, Colorado, Idaho, and Utah granted women the right to vote as well.

THINK ABOUT IT

On the frontier, women had to work as hard as men to survive. Do you think that may have helped them win voting rights?

Wyoming's state seal shows its commitment to equality for all.

PRESIDENTIAL SUPPORT

As women's suffrage slowly spread through the states, national support was needed. It was important that the whole country be united in standing up for women's rights. In 1917, a group of female **protestors** demonstrated outside of the White House. They were arrested and locked up. When they refused to

Women suffragists gathered to stand up for their rights at the White House.

President Wilson was convinced by the protestors to support women's suffrage.

eat, as a protest against being jailed, they were force-fed by the guards.

The president, Woodrow Wilson, had never been a big supporter of women's suffrage. This event changed his mind. In 1918, near the end of World War I, he gave a speech to Congress about it. Wilson said, "We have made partners of the women in this war." He asked Congress to pass an amendment to the Constitution to grant women the right to vote, to include women in "a partnership of privilege and right."

Victory for Women

The following year, in 1919, Congress passed the 19th Amendment and sent it to the states for **ratification**. In order for the amendment to be added to the Constitution, three-quarters of the states had to approve it. By August of 1920, thirty-six states had ratified the amendment. On August 26 the amendment officially became part of the Constitution.

The 19th amendment reads:

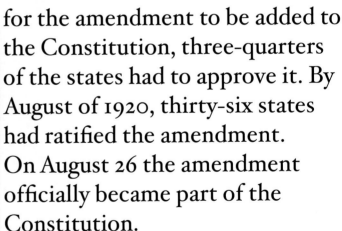

Suffragists, such as Alice Paul, toasted the ratification of the 19th Amendment.

The right of citizens of the United States to vote shall not be denied or abridged by the United States or by any state on account of sex.

Congress shall have power to enforce this article by appropriate legislation.

The struggles of U.S. suffragists for nearly a century were over, ended by these two sentences. The first sentence means that no one may stop a woman from voting just because she is a woman. The second says that Congress can pass more laws to make sure that no one is stopped from voting for that reason.

Women were finally able to cast their ballots in elections across the country.

Women's Suffrage Worldwide

In several countries women were allowed to vote before 1920. New Zealand was the first nation to give women the right to vote, in 1893. Canada, the United States' neighbor, granted most women the right in 1918. The United Kingdom had a large suffrage movement like that in the United States. Women over 30 years old gained the right to vote there in 1918. Younger

Emmeline Pankhurst and her daughter Christabel were British suffragists.

Women in Kuwait won the right to vote in 2005 and voted for the first time in 2006. ▶▶

women were not able to vote until 1928.

Women in most other countries gained suffrage by the end of the 1900s. South Africa allowed white women to vote in 1930, but people of other races couldn't vote until 1994. In 2015, Saudi Arabian women were able to vote for the first time, though only in some elections. Today, nearly all women around the world have the right to vote.

THINK ABOUT IT

Why is it important that all people have the right to vote?

CHALLENGES AHEAD

Women's struggles were not over once they had the right to vote. Over the last hundred years, women have continued to fight to be treated equally.

Women have fought for daycare, better education, and control over their lives. Many people worked to write an Equal Rights Amendment for the Constitution. The United States Senate passed the amendment in 1972, but it was not ratified by the states so it did not become law.

This 1978 march was in support of the Equal Rights Amendment.

Today, women still have to fight for equality in the United States.

Today, women still experience some discrimination. Modern issues include preventing abuse and guaranteeing equal pay for both sexes. Women in the United States today have the power to change laws to make their lives better because of the 19th Amendment.

GLOSSARY

abolitionist A person who is against slavery.

accurate Correct, free from mistakes.

advocate A person who stand ups for what they believe in.

centennial A celebration of the 100th anniversary of an event.

constitution A set of rules that guides how a country, state, or other organization works.

decade A period of ten years.

distinction Seeing or acting on differences.

document A paper with written or printed information.

exercise To put into use.

frontier An area on the edge of the settled part of a country; a frontier is often wild and rough.

injustice Something that is unfair.

liberation Being set free.

mock To make fun of something or someone.

motto A saying that represents what a group believes.

politician A person who runs for and serves in office.

research To carefully study something to learn more about it.

resolution A statement of one's feelings or opinions.

sentence To hand down a punishment.

sentiment Feeling or thought.

suffrage The right to vote.

suffragist A person fighting for the right to vote, especially for women's voting rights.

universal For or having to do with everyone.

For More Information

Books

Belviso, Meg and Pam Pollack. *Who Was Susan B. Anthony?* New York: Grosset & Dunlap, 2014.

Isecke, Harriet. *Women's Suffrage: Fighting for Women's Rights.* Huntington Beach, CA: Teacher Created Materials, 2011.

Nardo, Don. *The Split History of the Women's Suffrage Movement.* Mankato, MN: Compass Point Books, 2014.

Peppas, Lynn. *Women's Suffrage.* Ontario, Canada: Crabtree Publishing Company, 2015.

Rappaport, Doreen. *Elizabeth Started All the Trouble.* New York: Disney-Hyperion, 2016.

Websites

Because of the changing nature of internet links, Rosen Publishing has developed an online list of websites related to the subject of this book. This site is updated regularly. Please use this link to access the list:

http://www.rosenlinks.com/LFO/19

INDEX